Kingdom Daughters: Encouraging, Empowering, and Uplifting the Woman God has Called

By Nicole Rowan

To:
The one who always believed in me, Rosella
My Love, Perris
My Savior, Jesus

The author wishes to thank the following:

Editors -
Chris Monohan: For your willingness to read these words over and over and give up your time freely.

Nicholas Howard: For being you and helping me capture the words that would penetrate hearts in the most profound ways.

Randy Crane: For your unbelievable servant's heart and encouragement to actually have this printed.

Design -
Chelcea Cummings/Cupples Designs: For sharing your talent, and all the beauty you brought to these pages. You are by far one of the most eloquent people I have ever met.

My Sister,

I have been praying for you for a long time now. I have prayed over the words that you will read and I have petitioned on behalf of you and asked the Lord to release encouragement and empowerment on each person who comes in contact with this devotional. I can not begin to tell you how many times my heart has broken for my sisters who feel oppressed, alone and not valued. It was because of the countless stories and tears cried by women of great faith that the Lord encouraged me to write this simple, yet powerful devotional for you. I wish that I could sit in your living room and speak these things over your life; remind you that you are the daughter of the KING! Remind you that you are loved by the highest God and remind you that the Holy Spirit dwells in you. Most of all I'd remind you that the gifts are not gender specific and whether you are a stay at home mom, student, coffee shop barista, sales representative, leading in the business world, working in ministry or searching for a job - YOU matter. My sister, you are important and you were born for such a time as this! I pray for the releasing of gifts and the freedom to use them. I also pray that after these 30 days you will feel encouraged, empowered and uplifted to walk in the fullness of Christ as he intended for you.

You were created to do Kingdom work. You are a...

PART 1

Worthy

"But strive first for the kingdom of God and his righteousness, and all these things will be given to you as well." Matthew 6:33

"Therefore, since we are surrounded by so great a cloud of witnesses, let us also lay aside every weight and the sin that clings so closely, and let us run with perseverance the race that is set before us, looking to Jesus the pioneer and perfecter of our faith, who for the sake of the joy that was set before him endured the cross, disregarding its shame, and has taken his seat at the right hand of the throne of God." Hebrews 12:1-2

Get ready my sister: The King is preparing something for you. I am confident as you seek first for the Kingdom of God that He is going to add things to your life you would have never imagined! I know you've probably heard that before, but this time I see a picture of Jesus standing in Heaven mightily reminding you that you are more, that you were born for more than the limits you have put on your life and the box you have put yourself and Jesus in. You are more than your history, more than your mistakes, even more than your day-to-day roles. It's time to allow the Divine Author to write a divine story, and you are the main character. This journey is going to be a transformation of the mind and heart. Begin by giving the Lord praise and thanking Him for what has passed and what is to come. Don't miss out on spending time with the King of the universe today. He is your main source and He will continue to fill you up and use you to impact the world for His Kingdom.

Questions to Ponder

Where do you need transformation when it comes to your mind and heart?

What are things you would have never imagined the Lord adding to your life?

How do you want to impact the world around you?

"Do not be conformed to this world, but be transformed by the renewing of your minds, so that you may discern what is the will of God—what is good and acceptable and perfect." Romans 12:2

"So God created humankind in his image, in the image of God he created them; male and female he created them." Genesis 1:27

Resist the temptation to believe what the world says of your worth. For you were not created by the world, but by the King of the world.

With each step you take today remember: You are a masterpiece. The old is gone and the new has come. As you connect more with the Father, you will become aware of His presence, and as you become more aware of His presence, you will realize that His Spirit will not live in someone that is not worthy of Him. Since you are, He resides with you! When you look in the mirror, what do you see? What thoughts run through your head? My sister, today I want to call out "false image," I want to smack negativity right in the face and remind you that our Jesus doesn't make anything ugly. You were made in the image of God and when you don't receive a compliment well, you are indirectly saying Jesus didn't make you lovely. See, how you see you is how you will see others; how you love you is how you will love others; and how you accept you is how you will accept others. It's time to start loving yourself and realizing that your worth is that of the highest King.

Questions to Ponder

In what areas have you allowed the world to tell you who you are?
What are three positive words that describe you?
What do you love about you?

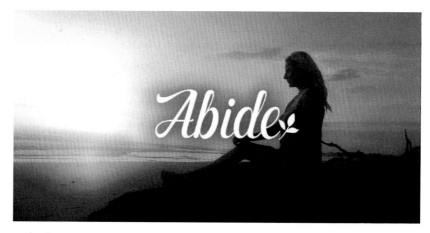

"Abide in me as I abide in you. Just as the branch cannot bear fruit by itself unless it abides in the vine, neither can you unless you abide in me." John 15:4

"You who live in the shelter of the Most High, who abide in the shadow of the Almighty, will say to the Lord, 'My refuge and my fortress; my God, in whom I trust.'" Psalm 91:1-2

Oh sister, how He loves you today and every day. He is pleased by you, and He loves when you abide in Him. The best part is when you spend time in His presence. He will lovingly tend to your fruit-bearing branches. As you abide in Him, He will abide in you and start to increase your fruit while cutting off old and dead branches. Dwelling is simply spending time with your perfect Creator. It can look a lot of different ways. Sometimes it's simply sitting and listening. Other times, it's worshiping your Maker and singing praises to Him. His desire is for you to have intimate fellowship with Him. Today my sister, dwell. Dwell in His everlasting love and faithfulness. Spend time with Him in the secret place and learn to move to His rhythm so that you can get through this day without any speed bumps. He is ready and willing to explode love all over your day and in every aspect of it!

Questions to Ponder

Block out all the distractions and spend some time in the presence of the Lord. Write down what He is saying to you and share with Him what you love about Him.

Restores Life

"Now when Jesus returned, the crowd welcomed him, for they were all waiting for him. Just then there came a man named Jairus, a leader of the synagogue. He fell at Jesus' feet and begged him to come to his house, for he had an only daughter, about 12 years old, who was dying. As he went, the crowds pressed in on him. Now there was a woman who had been suffering from hemorrhages for twelve years; and though she had spent all she had on physicians, no one could cure her. She came up behind him and touched the fringe of his clothes, and immediately her hemorrhage stopped. Then Jesus asked, 'Who touched me?' When all denied it, Peter said, 'Master, the crowds surround you and press in on you.' But Jesus said, 'Someone touched me; for I noticed that power had gone out from me.' When the woman saw that she could not remain hidden, she came trembling; and falling down before him, she declared in the presence of all the people why she had touched him, and how she had been immediately healed. He said to her, 'Daughter, your faith has made you well; go in peace.'" Luke 8:40-48

I love when Jesus heals people. More importantly, I love when He heals the people who culture has already deemed "rubbish." The woman He heals in Luke 8:40-48 is one of my favorites because Jesus surpasses all human understanding and a miracle is performed. For 12 years this lady suffered. She was rejected and at her wits' end when she heard about Jesus. Risking her life by going out into public, she knew if she could just touch Jesus' garment, she would be healed. It was because of her tenacious determination and faith that she would be healed. This woman had every reason to be discouraged and depressed, but instead she went out *looking* for Jesus. My sister, His garment is still available, He hasn't forgotten about you, He loves to heal His children. Sometimes His healing looks differently then what we want, but He knows what He is doing. Will you go out looking for the Miracle Maker today?

Questions to Ponder

What stood out for you when reading the story of the woman in Luke 8:40-48?
List out any areas of your life where you need healing from the Father?

"Therefore, I tell you, her sins, which were many, have been forgiven; hence she has shown great love. But the one to whom little is forgiven, loves little." Luke 7:47

"If we confess our sins, he who is faithful and just will forgive us our sins and cleanse us from all unrighteousness." 1 John 1:9

Today's word comes from a pit where a lot of my pain has drawn out; the place where I have stopped, and lingered for far too long; the place where I realized I was drowning in my past mistakes and where I assumed I was far beyond any help.

My sister, I assume that maybe you know this place as well. It's the place that you may only frequent in the dark of a cold night, where you have second-guessed the Lord's forgiveness. You've thought yourself too much of a mess and disregarded the Lord for what He has already done. But then, as you sit in your puddle of tears, you remember Mary Magdalene in the circle of people who awaited her stoning. As always, the only prince worthy of a bedtime love story changes the storyline. Instead of what you deserve, you get grace and love and forgiveness. He makes all things new, my sister: even you. Forgiveness is available, no matter what you've done. Nothing is too big for our Daddy. If there is something holding you back, lay it at His feet and ask Him to take it. Today, release shame, doubt, sins and unforgiveness to Him, the One who can make you white as snow.

Questions to Ponder

Where have you experienced a lot of grace?
What have you been holding onto that you need to release to the Father today?

"Be still before the LORD, and wait patiently for him; do not fret over those who prosper in their way, over those who carry out evil devices." Psalm 37:7

"Be still, and know that I am God! I am exalted among the nations, I am exalted in the earth." Psalm 46:10

My sister, spend a moment basking in the presence of the Lord and allow yourself to stand still before the rush of the world notices you are available. Take a deep breath, and then exhale all things that do not belong in the temple of Christ.

Today let's bring all our worries and discouragements to the table and rip them into pieces, for they don't belong in our thoughts or hearts anymore. Even in the midst of a busy schedule or the weight that this life sometimes carries, stillness can be found. Clarity can be given and strength can be renewed. Notice the word "know" in Psalm 46:10–it is an intimate word. It is full of trust and extremely involved. If you *know* Jesus, you will want to sit with Him, listen and be still before Him. He is the creator of all things and He holds the answer to all things. Since knowing Jesus, you have new standards in your life: freedom and peace. You can have stillness by putting guards (boundaries) around your heart so that nothing is allowed to disrupt the peace within you. You are powerful, and nothing about today can move that unless you let it.

Questions to Ponder

Where could you use some strength renewed in your life?
What kind of boundaries does your heart need to have in order
for peace to flow?

"You are the light of the world. A city built on a hill cannot be hid." Matthew 5:14

"You have been born anew, not of perishable but of imperishable seed, through the living and enduring word of God." 1 Peter 1:23

My sister, who you are is not defined by what others say of you. It is defined by the covenant you have with the Father. The truth is written in Scripture.

Here is a spoken word poem I wrote to remind you of who you are in Christ:

That I am a daughter of a king, forgiven and redeemed.
In His eyes, I am called blameless and clean.
the result of a broken lie,
and a forgiving tie from the King of Kings
That I am set free;
a new creation, chosen and no longer bound by the forbidden tree
I am led down the righteous **path,** breaking the <u>chains</u> of Satan's wrath.
That I am the light of the world, delivered, called and complete.
He has written "paid" all over my receipt
I am redeemed from the curse of sin, sickness, and poverty **bathed** in His everlasting sovereignty
And Jesus says that I am worth dying on the cross for, because <u>I am</u> simply worth more.

Questions to Ponder

Make a list of things the world has called you, and then another list of things that Jesus calls you.
Do you believe that you have been redeemed?

Obsession

"Hear, O Israel: The Lord is our God, the Lord alone. You shall love the Lord your God with all your heart, and with all your soul, and with all your might. Keep these words that I am commanding you today in your heart. Recite them to your children and talk about them when you are at home and when you are away, when you lie down and when you rise. Bind them as a sign on your hand, fix them as an emblem on your forehead, and write them on the doorposts of your house and on your gates." Deuteronomy 6:4-9

My sister, I pray that you would be obsessed with our Jesus, because He is obsessed with you! His love for you is never limited and never ceasing. Today, He wants all of your attention. He wants you to feel surrounded by His glory and His presence. Set your eyes on Him and think only of things that bring Him honor. You can experience Jesus in so many different ways today, He is no different than a friend you spend time with. Jesus is the most irresistible person to exist. At the cross, He removed the blocks that made it nearly impossible to have an intimate relationship with Him. There is going to be laughing, crying, closeness and bursts of freedom. This relationship is going from glory to glory and nothing can separate you from it. On top of it all, this love doesn't know what fear is. His attention is so much on you there is no room for anything else but perfect connection. Enter into a love obsession with the Prince of Peace and allow Him to overwhelm you with His thoughts. You will notice an increase in your joy and ability to face every day with a genuine excitement. Let today be that day that you enter into this intimate, loving, vulnerable relationship with Jesus.

Questions to Ponder

Take a moment and write a love letter thanking your Father for all He has done and will do.

Hiding

"No one after lighting a lamp puts it in a cellar, but on the lampstand so that those who enter may see the light." Luke 11:33

Come on out, my sister. Join me by presenting yourself for all to see. You are more than your title. You don't have to hide behind your profession as if that is all you are.

Revealing your light means revealing you. It means being you in every place you are, at all times. It means you're not ashamed of who you are, and surely not ashamed of Who lives within you. Whether you are a stay-at-home mom, student, boss, clerk, etc. your purpose in life does not change because of what you do. Your story matters and your past matters. Stop hiding it and go be a light to the world by declaring that over others' lives! Everything about you is beautiful, because you are beautifully and wonderfully made. Today, you have the ability to introduce the light (Christ) to a neighbor, co-worker or boss. Read that again, *YOU have the ability.* Not because you have a degree in theology or because you have all the answers. But because you have the light of the world: You have Christ in you and because of Him, you are able. I love how the verse starts off, "no one *after lighting* a lamp..." When you interact with Jesus and know Him intimately, you won't want to hide your faith or hide your love for Him!

Questions to Ponder

Have you been hiding in any areas of your life?
Do you believe that you have the ability to be a light? Where might you want to shine brighter?

Worthy of Praise

"Finally, beloved, whatever is true, whatever is honorable, whatever is just, whatever is pure, whatever is pleasing, whatever is commendable, if there is any excellence and if there is anything worthy of praise, think about these things." Philippians 4:8

"You were taught to put away your former way of life, your old self, corrupt and deluded by its lusts, and to be renewed in the spirit of your minds, and to clothe yourselves with the new self, created according to the likeness of God in true righteousness and holiness." Ephesians 4:22-24

My sister, when we allow our minds and thoughts to wander off on things that are not worthy of praise, they are not worthy of Jesus. We give power to negativity and fall back into the world's way of thinking. When we praise Jesus we remind ourselves of the greatness of God and His presence. The reason Paul is giving these instructions is the cross offers a brand new way of living; a hopeful way of living, a new covenant. It was such a radical change of living infused with so much hope it was a literal shock to many that heard it. Worthy belief makes worthy thinking, worthy thinking makes worthy actions, worthy actions birth worthy emotions to confirm what you're doing in life is unto the King. Recognizing how much He is involved in your world creates an appetite to release anything else left inside your heart to Him. Praise leads you into the courts of justice, where you will experience revelation, wisdom and understanding of what is around you and Who is in you.

Questions to Ponder

Take a moment and praise Jesus. Then share with Him all the areas of your life that you are hopeful.
Write down names of people or circumstances where you would like more hope.

PART 2

Purpose

Walking in Authority

"The seventy returned with joy, saying, 'Lord, in your name even the demons submit to us!' He said to them, 'I watched Satan fall from heaven like a flash of lightning. See, I have given you authority to tread on snakes and scorpions, and over all the power of the enemy; and nothing will hurt you.'" Luke 10:17-19

"And Jesus came and said to them, 'All authority in heaven and on earth has been given to me.'" Matthew 28:18

Every place you go today, Jesus goes there also! With each step you take, you are walking with the power and authority of Jesus Christ. The reality is, you walk with this ability because Christ walks with you and you are founded in Jesus. His anointing is on you in such a way that with faith you are able to rebuke the storms in your life as well as rebuking and overcoming the naysayers in your life. Take note of the word "all" that Jesus uses in Matthew 28. If Jesus has *all* of the authority and *all* of the power, than that means something or someone else has no authority or power. Because of this, no person, no situation, no emotion or information has more authority or power over you. That's GREAT news, sister! Jesus wants you to take your position of authority and stand firm in what He has already secured for you.

Questions to Ponder

What "storms" in your life do you need to rebuke today?
What do you think it means when Scripture says Jesus has "all" the authority?

"I'll instruct you and teach you the way you should go; I will counsel you with my eye upon you. Do not be like a horse or a mule, without understanding, whose temper must be curbed with bit and bridle, else it will not stay near you." Psalm 32:8-9

"Like newborn infants, long for the pure, spiritual milk, so that by it you may grow into salvation— if indeed you have tasted that the Lord is good." 1 Peter 2:2-3

The Lord speaking through the Psalmist is encouraging His readers that one can spiritually grow in their walk with Him; that He will council you and watch over you, because He loves His daughters. But like a child aging, there are always "growing pains." They are not meant to hurt you or harm you, but to strengthen you and make you aware that He is helping you grow. It will be in those times that your character and leadership will be tested. But sister, I ask that you lean into those growing pains, for I believe the Lord is doing something in and through you during those times. His desires for you are good and lovely, and He wants His daughters to grow in all areas of life. Resist the temptation to dwell on the spurts of pain that come along and think about growing into who God has called you to be.

Questions to Ponder

Where do you feel that you are growing as a daughter in Christ? Where would you like to be in 1 year? Career, fitness, personal life, etc.?

"My child, do not forget my teaching, but let your heart keep my commandments; for length of days and years of life and abundant welfare they will give you. Do not let loyalty and faithfulness forsake you; bind them around your neck, write them on the tablet of your heart so you will find favor and good repute in the sight of God and of people." Proverbs 3:1-4

"Let the favor of the Lord our God be upon us, and prosper for us the work of our hands—O prosper the work of our hands!" Psalm 90:17

Too often we look for favor from our bosses, our co-workers, and our friends. But the only favor that will fulfill us comes from God. He places the highest favor on our lives and He is our biggest fan! His dying on the cross and grace on our lives are just two examples of His love towards us. He has covered us with His blood and poured out His spirit and favor to help bring the Kingdom of God to the earth through you! Many people might speak flowery words about you, but these can't even compare to the words of the Lord for you. He is the promoter, He is the provider, He is the King of power! He is the God who hands out unmerited favor to His children. Today, make a promise to move from your human reasoning to the spiritual knowledge that God's view of you is pretty amazing.

Questions to Ponder

Who in your life has given you the highest compliment?
Take a look at Scripture and write down a few descriptive words
that Lord uses to describe you, then declare them over your life.

"As for you, the anointing that you received from him abides in you, and so you do not need anyone to teach you. But as his anointing teaches you about all things, and is true and is not a lie, and just as it has taught you, abide in him." 1 John 2:27

"The Spirit of the Lord is upon me, because he has anointed me to bring good news to the poor. He has sent me to proclaim release to the captives and recovery of sight to the blind, to let the oppressed go free, to proclaim the year of the Lord's favor."
Luke 4:18-19

God's anointing has everything to do with faith and the willingness to receive it and believe it. My sister, His anointing abides in you and is ready to be activated with your belief. Because of Christ in you, you have the power to deliver good news, proclaim the releasing of captives, heal the blind and set people free all in the name of Jesus! Binding up the broken hearted means restoring shattered minds. Right now you have that ability on you to do so: for your own mind as well as your family, loved ones and so forth. No one is safe from a blessing and everyone is looking for love with no conditions. You have been given the key to kingdom ministry, it's time to walk down that hallway with confidence and use it! The world awaits you, my friend.

Questions to Ponder

When you think of God's anointing abiding in you what comes to mind?

Write down the names of three people you would like to bless this week.

"Now to him who by the power at work within us is able to accomplish abundantly far more than all we can ask or imagine, to him be glory in the church and in Christ Jesus to all generations, forever and ever. Amen." Ephesians 3:20-21

"The thief comes only to steal and kill and destroy. I came that they may have life, and have it abundantly." John 10:10

Abundantly more, my sister, abundantly more! Notice the word *more* in the Ephesians verse—our God is able and capable of doing abundantly <u>more</u> than all we could ask or imagine. So often we limit our passions and our dreams because of the fear and doubt that surround us. All throughout the Bible, Jesus promises us a life far greater than what we could come up with ourselves.

Sister, you are needed for the kingdom of God, and He needs you to believe that! God wants you to walk in His fullness and operate in your gifting but you must be willing to believe what He has said of you even when your timing is different than His. Remember, 25 years passed before God fulfilled His promise to give Sarah and Abraham a baby. But God always does what He says He will do! Today, believe He has *more* for you, not necessary more material items or worldly things, but *more* for your calling! In fact, will you take a moment and write down the passions you believe God has given you? Start asking Jesus questions about the how, when, what and who God wants to set this up with. He doesn't give us the desires of our hearts for us to "sit" on them. Aren't you the least bit curious to find out what He has put in your heart?

Questions to Ponder

What passions came to mind when you read this devotional?
How, when, what and who:
What is a BIG dream of yours that you would like to see flourish?

Looking Forward

"Beloved, I do not consider that I have made it my own; but this one thing I do: forgetting what lies behind and straining forward to what lies ahead, I press on toward the goal for the prize of the heavenly call of God in Christ Jesus." Philippians 3:13-14

"Let your eyes look directly forward, and your gaze be straight before you. Keep straight the path of your feet, and all your ways will be sure. Do not swerve to the right or to the left; turn your foot away from evil." Proverbs 4:25-27

I declare right now that you are a sister who is going to look forward. Gone are the days of looking back over your shoulder at what has passed and what has tried to steal a piece of your heart. Your focus is on Jesus and you don't need to look back anymore. You are going to be known for being a symbol of hope of things to come. Moving forward from painful experiences will come easier because of your reliance on Jesus. Your excitement for the future will write stories of redemption on the lives of others. You are a woman of the future. Today will mark a significant chapter in your life story, because you no longer wear your past like a heavy pair of earrings. Instead, you walk with a confidence that is excited for what lies ahead, and you know Jesus will guide you and keep you on the right path. Today we are getting a divorce from shame, guilt and fear. Say, "Shame, guilt, and fear, I renounce every agreement I have made with you and I cancel them off my life. You all are to leave right now in Jesus name." Now say, "Holy Spirit, fill me with hope." And when you're done with that, do it again, and again and again and again. Now say, "Jesus, right now I forgive myself and all those who have wronged me for all they have done, said, didn't do and didn't say. I release them, and they do not owe me anything." Have fun dreaming, my sister.

Questions to Ponder

How did it feel when you forgave those who wronged you?
What are you excited for when you think of the future?

Opposition to Opportunity

"So we do not lose heart. Even though our outer nature is wasting away, our inner nature is being renewed day by day. For this slight momentary affliction is preparing us for an eternal weight of glory beyond all measure, because we look not at what can be seen but at what cannot be seen; for what can be seen is temporary, but what cannot be seen is eternal." 2 Corinthians 4:16-18

"See, I am sending you out like sheep into the midst of wolves; so be wise as serpents and innocent as doves." Matthew 10:16

Opposition from others will surely come your way, especially when you begin to walk in what God has called you to. But sister, opposition doesn't have enough power in your life to keep you distracted from Jesus and your assignment. Nobody else in the entire world has been given the same divine destiny as you, and you can stand tall in the face of naysayers. You are filled with love and the Holy Spirit, which means opposition and negativity have zero authority in your life. Instead of getting frustrated and allowing anger to take hold of your heart, remind yourself to look at others the way Jesus would: full of grace. You know the saying, "Hurt people, hurt people," but you also know that Jesus heals and wants to pour out His love like a rushing waterfall on His children. You are being sent out, but you do not lose heart for God is renewing you day by day. You have been entrusted to live out your life in a specific way, I pray right now that when such opposition comes your way, you will be ready to laugh at it and continue doing good work for a good God.

Questions to Ponder

Has opposition stopped you from going after what God placed on your heart?

Do you believe that God has placed a divine destiny on your life?

Rising Up

"Therefore, my beloved, be steadfast, immovable, always excelling in the work of the Lord, because you know that in the Lord your labor is not in vain." 1 Corinthians 15:58

"And she said, 'I will surely go with you; nevertheless, the road on which you are going will not lead to your glory, for the LORD will sell Sisera into the hand of a woman.' Then Deborah got up and went with Barak to Kedesh." Judges 4:9

In the book of Judges, our sister Deborah sets a pretty great standard for what it means to rise up and lead. Not every woman is necessarily called to be in lead positions, but there are times when God needs well-equipped believers to stand up and get to the front lines. Did you know that because of who God has created you to be, you are able to rise up and be the example of a passionate and confident leader? Even though God has been known to use people that are least likely to be promoted, you are all that you need to be in Him. I don't think He is looking for the degree or the title to bump you up. I think He is looking for the person who, no matter what, will believe who God says they are and what He says about them. You can stand and rise to the occasion, sister! You are whole and complete in Jesus, and He sees you as ready!

Questions to Ponder

Does being a leader scare you? If so, why? If not, where do you see yourself leading in the next year?

Detoxing

"Since we have these promises, beloved, let us cleanse ourselves from every defilement of body and of spirit, making holiness perfect in the fear of God." 2 Corinthians 7:1

"The good person out of the good treasure of the heart produces good, and the evil person out of evil treasure produces evil; for it is out of the abundance of the heart that the mouth speaks." Luke 6:45

My sister, detoxing is surveying what you have, and where you want to be. It's recognizing who you want to become. It's changing from protecting your heart to guarding it. Self-protection has fear attached to it, it's afraid of hurt, it's threatened by people or situations, but people have never been our enemy and they never will be.

It's time to DTR (define the relationship) with who is in your life and where you are. It's wise to get confirmation and clarity with what you are to be involved with and what you are not to be. Sister, not everyone is a long-term friend, some people are connected for a season, some are a branch who will eventually get trimmed, and some are in our roots, lifelong. Detoxing our lives, hearts and minds helps us focus on God's specific purpose for us. When we are able to recognize things in our life that do not deserve our attention, we become more aware of the things that do.

Questions to Ponder

Take a quick survey of your life. Are you satisfied? What, if anything, would you like to change?
Where do you think detoxing needs to take place in your life?

"Therefore, since we are receiving a kingdom that cannot be shaken, let us give thanks, by which we offer to God an acceptable worship with reverence and awe; for indeed our God is a consuming fire." Hebrews 12:28-29

"He said to him, 'You shall love the Lord your God with all your heart, and with all your soul, and with all your mind.'" Matthew 22:37

Today is the day, my sister! I'm praying specifically that our God, who is a consuming fire, will awaken your heart and overwhelm you like a fire overwhelms its location. Unlike a candle, which is confined to a specific vase, our God is like a raging fire that cannot be controlled or contained. We cannot be separated from the love of the Father. He is a devoted lover and wants to consume all of you. Not half of you, not 10 percent of you, but ALL of you. He loves you and wants you to be filled completely! His desire is that you would "catch the flame and help light others;" that you would be so filled with the Holy Spirit that others would notice by just watching you. Whether it's behind a desk, serving at a restaurant, or laboring after children, wherever your work may be today, may you be a consuming fire of love in the name of Jesus.

Questions to Ponder

Why is it that so many people are attracted to fires? What do you think it is that catches the eye?
How might that relate to the love of the Father?

PART 3

Calling

"The Lord is my light and my salvation; whom shall I fear? The Lord is the stronghold of my life; of whom shall I be afraid?" Psalm 27:1

"So if anyone is in Christ, there is a new creation: everything old has passed away; see, everything has become new!" 2 Corinthians 5:17

Too many times you have passed through the battlefields of bad news, letdowns and disappointments, but this time you see something different. You declare you will not give up by sitting down—legs crossed and arms up in forfeit—because you realize that you are not alone and that He is with you at all times. Even in the darkest moments you can bring light because He is in you and He is light. You also realize that your strength is not enough, but that He adores you and believes that you can get through anything with Him. He is the best lawyer you could have and He always succeeds. You make up His team, and like any good father He is always ready to go before and defend His daughter. My sister, what if this time is not like the last? What if I told you that your past does not have to be your future and that you are not your mistakes? What if the rejection you feel didn't control you like you think it does? What now would you do with your time, talents and treasures? You are starting to understand who you are in Christ. You won't be a daughter who is tossed to and fro. You will take a deep breath, look to Jesus sitting on the throne, and in full reliance ask your Father, "What now, Papa?"

Questions to Ponder

What has God made new in your life over the past 3 years?
When you think of the future, what are you ready for?

A Pleased Father

"For the Lord takes pleasure in his people; he adorns the humble with victory." Psalm 149:4

"But God proves his love for us in that while we still were sinners Christ died for us." Romans 5:8

"For God so loved the world that he gave his only Son, so that everyone who believes in him may not perish but may have eternal life." John 3:16

There is nothing in the world, my sister, that you can do to make God not love you. He loves his children so much and wants you to know that today! When you feel like you don't measure up to those around you or you think your job is not as glamorous as it could be, simply rest in the Father's love for you. In Him, you are royalty, you are a prized possession, and He lavishes His love upon you. His approval is within your reach and you have the full benefit of receiving it every day. He proved His dying love (literally) for you when His blood was shed for you at Calvary. He is a Father who is well-pleased with you. When He sees you, He sees the best version, the best little child of Him. He wants you to start seeing yourself like He sees you because it is a beautiful, explosive love of a sight. Even while you were in your dirty, messy sin, He died because He loved you.

Now go, my sister, and live knowing that you have permission to be yourself and only you. Being anyone else is boring. You simply being you is what the world needs.

Questions to Ponder

Do you know that the Father sees us as His prized possession?
What is your most prized possession?
What does the best version of you look like?

Ambassador

"But be doers of the word, and not merely hearers who deceive themselves. For if any are hearers of the word and not doers, they are like those who look at themselves in a mirror; for they look at themselves and, on going away, immediately forget what they were like. But those who look into the perfect law, the law of liberty, and persevere, being not hearers who forget but doers who act—they will be blessed in their doing." James 1:22-25

"And whatever you do, in word or deed, do everything in the name of the Lord Jesus, giving thanks to God the Father through him." Colossians 3:17

You no longer want to sit back and watch, but you are ready to "get in the game" and play. You know what you are supposed to do and you've been given good things from the Lord to accomplish all that He wants to do through you. You are highly needed and greatly gifted. It's because of your love for Jesus that you operate out of His love for others. You see this opportunity as a privilege and honor and are compelled to do whatever is needed to see the Kingdom of God flourish. Go, my sister, and help bring the Kingdom of God to all that surrounds you. You are an important ambassador and all of heaven is cheering you on! Your sluggish ways are thrown out, your hesitation is gone and you are ready to kiss the earth with love, hope and Jesus.

Questions to Ponder

What do you think an ambassador should look like? How should they act?

How can you help the Kingdom of God flourish here on earth?

"Keep these words that I am commanding you today in your heart. Recite them to your children and talk about them when you are at home and when you are away, when you lie down and when you rise." Deuteronomy 6:6-7

"Death and life are in the power of the tongue, and those who love it will eat its fruits." Proverbs 18:21

Your words have power, my sister! The things you say to yourself and others can build up or tear down. Be a speaker of love today and allow the fruit of the spirit to flow from your heart and spill off your lips. God spoke the world into existence and since you are made in the image of God you, too, can speak things to life. Speaking death is not who you are because Christ resides in you. When the world gets the best of you and starts to drag you down, remember the words that God has spoken about you and for you. They are words of love and honor; words of value and reassurance. As you embark on another day, declare God's word over your life.

You carry a love weapon, and it's all in the way you speak, so speak words of life and truth.

Questions to Ponder

What are a few declarations you can make over your life today? Write down an encouraging word you have received from a friend in the past few months.

"My frame was not hidden from you, when I was being made in secret, intricately woven in the depths of the earth. Your eyes beheld my unformed substance. In your book were written all the days that were formed for me, when none of them as yet existed. How weighty to me are your thoughts, O God! How vast is the sum of them!" Psalm 139: 15-17

"Before I formed you in the womb I knew you, and before you were born I consecrated you; I appointed you a prophet to the nations." Jeremiah 1:5

YOU ARE COMMISSIONED AND CALLED, MY SISTER! Every ounce of your passion to see Christ known is not to be hidden.

He has summoned you by name, you are His creation! Rise up! I say again, rise up and go forth using the gifts He has given you. You are able, believe it! Walk in the truth that the Father sends you and is with you, always. There is no one else in the world like you. If you don't press into who Christ has made you to be, then the world misses out. You have a purpose, my sister; a reason why you were created. Your days were written down already; your name written in the palm of His hands and in the book of life. Everything with God has purpose all over it. The dreams and desires within you are not random, they are actually busting to get out. You are equipped to see these dreams not only happen, but to go beyond what you ask, think or imagine. There is no lie or excuse that can disqualify any person in Jesus from fulfilling what they are called to do. My sister, what are you dreaming about today?

Questions to Ponder

What do you believe your purpose is?
When you think that God made you specifically for a purpose, how does that change your view on everyday living?

"For we walk by faith, not by sight." 2 Corinthians 5:7

"Now faith is the assurance of things hoped for, the conviction of things not seen." Hebrews 11:1

The distractions of this world cannot hold you back from being with Jesus. When we fully rely on the Lord and follow Him simply because He is our Papa, He is very honored. Sometimes we don't always understand why He calls us into certain seasons, job changes and relocations. But we know our faithful Daddy, which means we know that even when seasons change, a new beauty arises. When we walk by faith, it simply means sitting in His presence and talking to Him as you would with a friend: believing He is who He says He is and what He says about you and your life is the truth. Hearing from God is normal, and you can hear from Him, sister. Your faith is linked to trust, and trust to love. This makes hearing God normal for you. Believing this will change your experience in every part of your life. You will soon begin to notice that the voices of stress, worry, and the past actually get annoying. Your Father has a permanent invitation called, "Come to me those who are _____," and He lists things in the way of Love. Have fun opening your invite today and enjoy your best conversation with God

Be encouraged: God is with you and will make a way as you continue to walk in faith and not by the sights of this life.

Questions to Ponder

Take a moment and have a conversation with your Papa and tell Him where you would like your faith to grow.
Did you hear anything back from Him? If so, write it down here.

"Pray then in this way: Our Father in heaven, hallowed be your name. Your kingdom come. Your will be done, on earth as it is in heaven. Give us this day our daily bread. And forgive us our debts, as we also have forgiven our debtors. And do not bring us to the time of trial, but rescue us from the evil one." Matthew 6:9-13

Take a seat, my sister and be encouraged as you think about what the day holds. Do not worry about yesterday or today, or what tomorrow will bring. Instead, trust that God is going to provide every need you have, for His love is all over you. He wants to be your ultimate provider, and your cornerstone. Take a moment and thank God for what He has already provided for you today. Just like the manna that was given to the Israelites while in the desert, sometimes we have just enough to get by each day. Entering into a "Heaven on Earth" reality does begin with thanksgiving. Thankfulness cultivates the atmosphere of Heaven on Earth within you and around you. Daily provision of all your needs is met and ready for you to obtain in every area of your life. Here is the deal, sister, your Father doesn't lead you into anything without providing what you need. Believe that today, my sister!

Questions to Ponder

Make a list of everything you are thankful for today and give your Father some praise.

"The one who enters by the gate is the shepherd of the sheep. The gatekeeper opens the gate for him, and the sheep hear his voice. He calls his own sheep by name and leads them out. When he has brought out all his own, he goes ahead of them, and the sheep follow him because they know his voice. They will not follow a stranger, but they will run from him because they do not know the voice of strangers." John 10:2-5

"'Father, glorify your name.' Then a voice came from heaven, 'I have glorified it, and I will glorify it again.' The crowd standing there heard it and said that it was thunder. Others said, 'An angel has spoken to him.' Jesus answered, 'This voice has come for your sake, not for mine.'" John 12:28-30

If you are reading this, you must be a woman who desires to hear the Lord. If you are anything like me, you love having a two-way conversation with your Papa and you live for that relationship with Him. Sometimes the Lord speaks to us so loudly we can't deny His voice. Other times He simply whispers. In John 12:30, Jesus points out that God's voice was not for His benefit—because He heard from God all the time—but it was for the disciples' faith. My sister, I hope to encourage you today that God's voice is powerful and perfect no matter how it is heard. Like a loving Father, He wants the best for His children. The Shepherd loves to lead His sheep down the right path because He knows what is best. Position yourself today and be ready to hear from your Shepherd. He holds your directions in His voice.

Questions to Ponder

How does the Lord speak to you?
How might you be able to position yourself to hear from Him more often?

I've written this spoken word poem so that you will be reminded how wonderful and brave you are in Christ. My sister, believe it today!

My sister, let's be brave together, rise above the culture and make the world a little bit better. For you were born for such a time as this.
For you were created by the King of kings, Lord of lords and He always makes beautiful things.
But you are more than just beautiful. You are brave and courageous. You encompass valor and your love for Jesus is contagious.
The strength and passion that you hold are gifts from the Maker whispering to you, "My daughter, Be bold."
Your character is impressive and one to speak of, your wisdom is seasoned and your heart is full of love.
You refuse to give up in times of darkness and pain, you seek the Kingdom of God and you know He reigns.
You are prayerful like Hannah, and faithful like Ruth. You sing songs of hope, redemption and truth.
Anointed and prepared, down a path God is taking you. He believes that you can stand strong because you been tried and found true.
You are a warrior like Deborah, who rescues those from oppression and, faithful like Sarah, you leave a Godly impression.
The Author of your story is not yet finished with your novel; He wants your name to go down with the brave women in the gospel.
Rise up, my sister, rise up I say, for Christ wants you to be brave today.

Questions to Ponder

What does bravery look like in your life?
As you read the spoken word poem, did you believe the words spoken about you?

"Then Jesus said to the Jews who had believed in him, 'If you continue in my word, you are truly my disciples; and you will know the truth, and the truth will make you free.'" John 8:31-32

"Indeed, we live as human beings, but we do not wage war according to human standards; for the weapons of our warfare are not merely human, but they have divine power to destroy strongholds. We destroy arguments and every proud obstacle raised up against the knowledge of God, and we take every thought captive to obey Christ." 2 Corinthians 10:3-5

The truth makes us free and freedom is the place where God wants you to reside. If you are feeling as if you can't walk in freedom, I want to tell you that our God is a God of deliverance. He is the God that sets captives and prisoners free! My sister, He wants you to be completely free in Him and His biggest desire is that you believe the truth. The truth that says He loves you, the truth that says you are worthy, and the truth that claims your authority. In the book of John, Satan is called the "thief" and you better believe that he wants to steal from you the truth that God has written over your life. But sister, you will not give Satan any authority. Those days are gone. You relinquish anything that is not true and anything that might prevent you from believing what God says about you. I declare that you will no longer believe the lies that Satan throws at you because when you empower it, it is allowed to stay on you. So in Jesus' name, today, you shake off anything you have believed in your past that is not of the holy and perfect God.

Questions to Ponder

Is there anything that you need deliverance from today?
Do you feel the freedom to be you and allow the Father to lavish
His love on you?

Powerful Reminders for Myself or Just Really Good Things to Note...